Amazing Nature

Marvelous Migrators

Tim Knight

Heinemann Library
Chicago, Illinois

a division of Reed Elsevier Inc.
Chicago, Illinois

Customer Service 888-454-2279

Visit our website at www.heinemannlibrary.com

Printed and bound in the Hong Kong, China by South China Printing

07 06 05 04 03
10 9 8 7 6 5 4 3 2 1

Library of Congress Cataloging-in-Publication Data

Knight, Tim.
　　Marvelous migrators / Tim Knight.
　　　p. cm. -- (Amazing nature)
　　Includes index.
　　Summary: Explores different ways that animals and insects migrate, from the powerful ruby-throated hummingbird that flies from Canada to Panama and back each year, to tiny spiders that go where the wind carries them.
　　ISBN 1-4034-1149-2 (hardcover) ISBN 1-4034-3260-0 (paperback)
　　1. Animal migration--Juvenile literature.　　[1. Animals--Migration.]　　I. Title.　II. Series: Knight. Tim. Amazing nature.
QL754.K55 2003
591.56'8--dc21

2002153005

Acknowledgments
The Publishers would like to thank the following for permission to reproduce photographs:
p. 4 Stephen Dalton/NHPA; p. 5 Jorg & Petra Wegner/Bruce Coleman; p. 6 Dr. Eckart Pott/ Bruce Coleman; p. 7 Heather Angel; p. 8 E & D Hosking/FLPA; p. 9 Steve Maslowski/FLPA; p. 10 Bill Coster/NHPA; p. 11 Pacific Stock/Bruce Coleman; p. 12 Jeff Goodman/NHPA; p. 13 Gunter Ziesler/Bruce Coleman; p. 14 Mark Newman/FLPA; p. 15 Bruce Coleman; pp. 16, 17 B & C Alexander/NHPA; p. 18 Terry Whittaker/FLPA; p. 19 P. David/FLPA; p. 20 Fred Bruemmer/Bruce Coleman; p. 21 Ardea; p. 22 Bruce Coleman; p. 23 Martin Harvey/NHPA; p. 24 Hellio and Van Ingen/NHPA; p. 25 Wayne Lawler/Corbis; p. 26 Roger Tidman/FLPA; p. 27 Anthony Bannister/NHPA.

Cover photo: Reproduced with permission of Tom Mangelsen/Nature Picture Library.

Every effort has been made to contact copyright holders of any material reproduced in this book. Any omissions will be rectified in subsequent printings if notice is given to the publisher.

Some words are shown in bold, **like this.** You can find out what they mean by looking in the glossary.

Contents

Mobile Homes

Some animals spend their whole lives in the same place. The place where animals live is their **habitat**. Others move to a new habitat at least once during their lifetime. Some **migrate** to different places at different times of the year. These movements to a new habitat are known as **migrations**.

Some animals migrate to find food or water. Others are looking for a safe place to raise a family. Some move to escape the cold. Others are trying to get away from the heat.

Most types of migrations are regular events. For example, every fall millions of birds in North America fly south. The **nectar,** insects, and meat the birds eat is harder to find at this time of year, so the birds fly to where there is more food. Every spring, the same birds travel back to their **breeding grounds** in the north. In Europe, many birds also fly south to escape the cold northern winter.

Twice a year, millions of European swallows migrate to and from South Africa across the Mediterranean Sea and the Sahara Desert.

Other movements do not follow any pattern. A bad **drought,** heavy rain, or an unexpected change in temperature can start a sudden large movement of animals.

Scientists are still discovering new facts about the amazing trips that some animals make. The story of animal migration is full of interesting facts and unsolved mysteries.

At the start of the rainy season, herds of zebras and gnus leave the dry, dusty plain. They head for places where the first new grass is beginning to grow.

Traveling Light

Most insects look too light and small to fly long distances. But do not let that fool you. For example, some butterflies never fly far from the place where they hatched, but others travel thousands of miles.

The North American monarch is the most famous butterfly that **migrates.** Every fall, hundreds of millions of monarchs fly up to 2,485 miles (4,000 kilometers) to escape the cold winter. Each year the butterflies follow exactly the same route. They only stop to rest at night, so they can cover more than 62 miles (100 kilometers) in a day. Their journey south ends in Mexico. Huge numbers of them **hibernate** there in a few favorite valleys. In spring they fly north again. This time they move more slowly. They feed and **mate** along the way. Most of them die before reaching their original home.

Hibernating monarch butterflies cling to the tree branches, bunching together to keep warm.

Large numbers of newly hatched bogong moths escape the summer heat by heading to Australia's highest mountain range. There they crawl into dark, cool cracks in the rocks. These areas get so crowded that thousands of moths spill out around the edges.

Young spiders migrate, too. They have no wings, so they turn themselves into tiny kites. They hang on to thin threads of their own silk. The threads and spider are swept into the air and carried away on the breeze. Using air **currents** in this way is known as "ballooning."

The bodies of bogong moths crowd into a shady spot high in the Australian Alps.

Free as a Bird

Birds are able to fly long distances. English swallows cross the burning Sahara Desert to their winter home in South Africa. On their fall **migration** to India, bar-headed geese from Tibet and demoiselle cranes from Siberia have to fly very high. To cross the Himalayas, the world's tallest mountains, they fly at heights over 3.4 miles (5.5 kilometers).

Arctic terns return to Antarctica every year. They split their time between the North and South Poles. Arctic terns enjoy two summers in a row by leaving each pole just before the dark winter sets in. With 24-hour sunshine throughout the year, the arctic tern sees more daylight than any other animal on Earth.

An arctic tern breaks its long trip from pole to pole by resting on the sea or perching on ice.

The mighty hummingbird

The migration of the ruby-throated hummingbird is quite amazing. It flies from Canada to Panama in Central America and back again. The tiny bird flies down through North America, stopping off along the way to feed on flowers. The quickest route into Central America is straight across the Gulf of Mexico. But crossing the sea is tricky, even for large birds. The ruby-throated hummingbird weighs only one-tenth of an ounce (three grams). But it flies straight across nearly 500 miles (800 kilometers) of open water. In fact, it risks its life to do this nonstop 18-hour flight!

A hummingbird on its long trip south stops briefly to refuel in midair.

Powered Flight

Long-distance flying uses up a lot of time and energy. Birds need to make sure that they have enough wing power to go the distance.

In the few weeks before it **migrates** from Europe to South Africa, the sedge warbler doubles its weight from 0.4 to 0.8 ounce (11 to 22 grams). This gives it enough energy to fly for 90 hours without a rest. Sandpipers and other small shorebirds also eat extra food before **migration**. Their brain and other organs shrink to make more room for the **fat reserves** that the birds need for the long trip ahead.

Heavy birds, such as geese, must fly quickly to stay in the air. This uses up lots of energy, so they need to stop many times to feed. They often fly during the night to keep cool.

Flocks of migrating geese, called skeins, fly in a "V" shape. Each bird takes a turn at the front, while the rest follow.

Riding the wind

Birds of prey, such as eagles, hawks, and turkey vultures, save energy by riding on **thermals.** These are **currents** of warm air that lift them high in the sky. They travel long distances by gliding slowly on the thermals. But there are no thermals over the sea. Birds flying from Europe to Africa try to cross the Mediterranean Sea at its narrowest point—the Strait of Gibraltar. Birds of prey normally live alone. But at migration time they crowd together in big groups to cross the sea at the same place.

Bald eagles often migrate in groups that spread out over 30 miles (50 kilometers).

Long-Distance Walkers

Walking long distances takes much more time than flying, so most land animals avoid long **migrations.** Some animals have no choice. They have to move to survive. For example, animals have to move if their food supply runs out or freezes over.

Caribou spend the summer feeding on moss and grass in the Arctic **tundra.** Before winter, the herds head south to look for food and a place to live in the forests. The biggest herds have nearly half a million animals. They travel up to 40 miles (65 kilometers) a day to escape the snow and freezing wind. As spring returns, they follow the same migration path back to their **breeding grounds,** some 600 miles (965 kilometers) away in the far north.

*Emus cannot fly, but they walk farther than any other bird. During **droughts,** emus walk up to 300 miles (483 kilometers) looking for water.*

Gnus struggle to climb the steep, muddy bank, blocking the escape route of the animals in the river behind them.

Plain travel

The largest herds of animals that **migrate** are found on the plains of East Africa. The most famous is the gnu. Twice every year, a million gnus and 200,000 zebras migrate. Their grassland home in Kenya begins to dry out, so they "follow the rains" to greener grass in Tanzania. Their pounding hooves kick up a trail of dust stretching for miles across the plain.

At one point along the way, the crocodile-filled Mara River blocks the gnus' path. There is a wild scramble to cross the flooded river. Thousands of gnus are drowned, crushed by others, or killed by hungry crocodiles. Six months later, those that lived make the same trip back.

Journeys Under the Sea

Animals that live in the ocean **migrate,** too. Northern elephant seals spend over half their lives traveling between California and the northern part of the Pacific Ocean. The trip back covers almost 12,000 miles (19,300 kilometers). It is the longest known **migration** for a **mammal.**

Humpback whales sing to each other during their long migrations. They travel from their **breeding grounds** to their winter feeding grounds. As they travel, their songs keep changing. Scientists still do not know the reason they do this.

Seals can swim long distances underwater, so their migration paths are not easy for scientists to study.

Sticking together

Spiny lobsters live in holes on **coral reefs** near the Bahamas. In fall, when it gets stormy, they gather together on the sandy sea bottom. Here they form long lines of 50 or more. Then they march off in single file. The lobsters head for deeper water. There they will be safe from the storms. But the deep water is much colder, which slows down the lobsters so that they use less energy. This helps them stay alive at a time when there is not much food. If the lobsters are in danger, they form a tight circle, with their heads facing outward. They fight off the enemy with their spiky **antennae**.

Spiny lobsters stick together for protection as they move across the sandy seafloor.

River Adventure

Salmon have to make one of nature's hardest **migrations.** Salmon spend most of their life in the ocean. When fully grown, they **migrate** hundreds of miles back to the river where they were born.

In late summer, they begin to gather around the coast of the ocean. Each salmon heads for the **estuary** that leads back to the river where it was born. Reaching the coast is the easy part. The real test comes when they begin to swim up the river.

The salmon have to fight against the strong **current.** In Alaska, migrating Pacific salmon have to dodge hungry brown bears. The bears hang around the "salmon leaps" waiting for an easy meal. Salmon also may have to get over waterfalls that block their path. To do this, the salmon jump out of the water by smashing their tails against the surface.

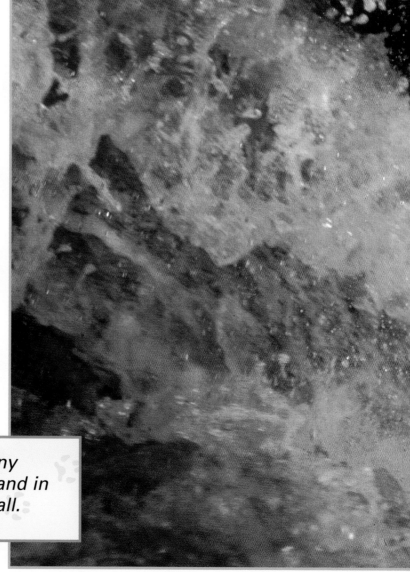

A salmon may have to make many tiring leaps before it can finally land in the calmer water above a waterfall.

Once in a lifetime

When the salmon finally reach the river where they were born, there is no time for rest. They must fight for a partner before they can **mate** and the females can lay eggs. Pacific salmon only make this hard journey once in a lifetime. They die after they **spawn**. They are too worn out to go back to the sea. The next spring the eggs hatch. The tiny salmon, known as fry, swim out to sea. A few years later the fully grown salmon will return to the same river to spawn.

Fish out of Water

Adult eels **migrate** huge distances when they are ready to **mate**. Many of these eels have grown up in rivers in Europe or North America. They leave these feeding grounds and swim thousands of miles to the Sargasso Sea. The Sargasso Sea is a part of the Atlantic Ocean northeast of the West Indies. The warm water in this sea is where the eels lay their eggs.

The newly hatched eels are called glass eels. They, too, have to make a long trip. The glass eels travel deep in the ocean. They are carried along by a strong **current** called the Gulf Stream. The trip takes many months.

By the time they have reached the coast of North America or Europe, they look like tiny copies of adult eels. They head straight for the nearest **estuary** and swim up the river. The eels stay close to the banks so they will not get swept back out to sea. To get around waterfalls, they crawl out of the water and wriggle along on land before sliding back in the river.

Newly hatched eels look like long, thin clear leaves. As they cross the Atlantic Ocean, their bodies change shape.

*Young eels gather together in a slithering, squirming ball. Their **migration** path up the river is blocked by a gate.*

The young eels live in freshwater for a few years. When they are old enough to mate, they make the long trip back to where they were born. They travel mainly at night. During the heat of the day they rest. They usually swim down the river to the sea, but they will crawl across damp fields if it is the quickest way back to the coast.

Once in the sea, the eels dive so deep that they disappear without a trace. Months later, they show up thousands of miles away in the Sargasso Sea. Here they **spawn** and die. Nobody really knows how they get there.

Yearly Visits

Eels and most salmon die as soon as they have **spawned.** But some animals go back to the same **breeding grounds** year after year.

Sea turtles spend most of their lives in the ocean. But they have to **migrate** back to the land to lay their eggs. Every **breeding season,** females crawl out of the ocean to the same stretch of sandy beach. There are only a few safe beaches left in the world, so the turtles do not have much choice about where to nest. On some of the most crowded beaches, huge numbers of female turtles arrive. In Costa Rica, more than 100,000 olive ridley turtles have been counted on one beach. They have to climb over each other to find a space.

A female olive ridley turtle drags her heavy body onto the beach.

A bright red tide of baby Christmas Island crabs floods past an adult and heads for the safety of the forest.

Land crabs only visit the sea to spawn. Every year on Christmas Island in the Indian Ocean, an amazing **migration** happens. The **monsoon** rains cause all the land crabs to migrate. In the rain, the crabs are safe from the hot sun. Around 120 million red crabs leave their forest homes and scurry down to the seashore. Their migration march cuts straight across roads and gardens. It is almost impossible to drive or walk anywhere on the island without crushing crabs.

The Wanderers

Some animals spend their whole lives on the move. They stop wherever they find a meal. They move on again as soon as the food runs out. This kind of movement follows no regular pattern. It is known as **nomadic migration.**

In the baking hot Australian desert, heavy rain may not fall for many years. When rain finally comes, it fills the dried-up lakes and rivers with water. Ducks **migrate** to these lakes and rivers from nowhere. **Dormant** seeds quickly sprout. Soon the bare ground is covered with flowering plants. Flocks of parakeets and other seed-eating parrots also migrate into the area to get in on the feast.

In very bad winters, large flocks of waxwing birds fly across the North Sea from Scandinavia. They flock to gardens in Great Britain and strip the red berries from firethorn and cotoneaster bushes. These sudden invasions, known as **irruptions,** only happen when the birds' normal food supply runs out.

In Australia, parakeets gather in flocks when desert plants burst into flower.

A giant flock of red-billed queleas can spell disaster for grain farmers.

Birds of a feather

Nomadic migrations are not always welcome. In Africa millions of red-billed queleas, a type of seed-eating songbird, often gather. They will travel up to 620 miles (1,000 kilometers) in search of food. A flying quelea flock looks like a huge swarm of insects. Normally, queleas feed on wild grass seed. But if their food supply runs out, they flock to farmland. A million queleas can eat a field of wheat in minutes.

Unwelcome Visitors

Every few years, some animals, especially insects, have more **offspring** than usual. When this happens, there is not enough food to go around. The new group of young has to move to a different area to find food and a new home. This is known as **removal migration.** In many cases, the newcomers cause problems.

Desert locusts are one of the most unwelcome visitors. They normally live in the driest parts of North Africa. From time to time they **mate** in huge numbers and **migrate** to other parts of the world. They destroy crops along the way. During the worst locust **plagues,** a swarm can spread out over an area of about 11 million square miles (28 million square kilometers).

Locusts that fly over the Red Sea cover about 200 miles (320 kilometers).

"Armyworm" is the name given to the caterpillars that migrate across farmland all around the world. They eat every bit of green plant life in their path. These marches, known as **infestations,** usually happen after a time of cold, wet weather. This is when armyworm enemies are less common. Infestations easily spread to new areas. This happens because armyworm caterpillars turn into moths that can travel more than 62 miles (100 kilometers) in one night.

Since they were brought to Australia, cane toads have spread quickly.

Sneaky travelers

Humans sometimes play a part in bringing animals that do not normally migrate to areas where they do not belong. Long ago, black rats sneaked onto boats and ships. Traveling this way, they reached almost every part of the planet. Black rats often drive out **native species** and take over their **habitat**. They may also spread diseases and harm crops.

Finding the Way

How do all these long-distance travelers find their way around? Tiny spiders and the weakest insects do not have much control over where they go. They end up wherever the wind carries them. Some birds follow landforms such as coastlines, valleys, and mountains. Other birds figure out where they are from where the Sun is in the sky. Those that fly at night use the stars. We know this because birds sometimes lose their way when the sky is cloudy.

Insects also use the Sun to find their way. The Sun keeps moving in the sky, so the **migration** path of most butterflies changes with the time of day they fly. But all monarch butterflies follow the same path, whatever time it is. They **migrate** in a straight line, using **magnetic** particles in their bodies to guide them.

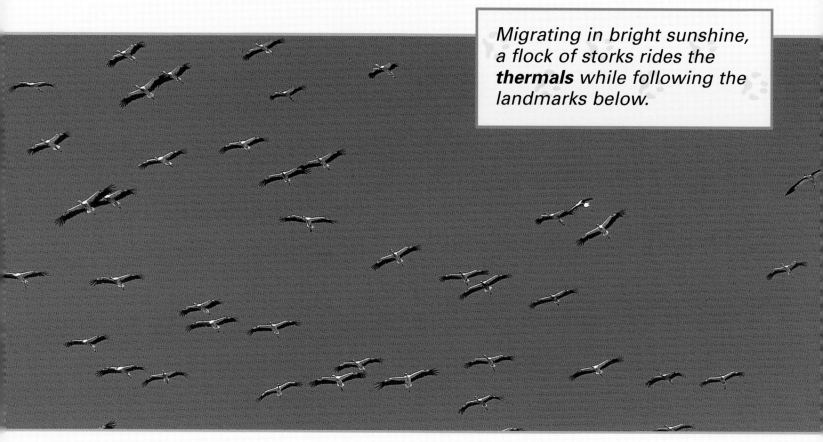

*Migrating in bright sunshine, a flock of storks rides the **thermals** while following the landmarks below.*

*Loggerhead turtles are born with a migration "map" inside their heads. When they hatch, baby loggerheads head for the sea. Mysteriously guided by the Earth's **magnetic field**, they start on a "swimathon" that may take ten years to complete. They travel alone, using the same migration path used by their parents. Even scientists cannot explain exactly how this is done.*

Fact File

The longest **migration** of all is made by the arctic tern. Each year it flies to Antarctica, a distance of more than 12,000 miles (19,000 kilometers).

In 1988, a swarm of desert locusts flew across the Atlantic Ocean from West Africa to the Caribbean. The 3,100-mile (5,000-kilometer) crossing took ten days. It is the longest known insect migration.

Wading birds migrating from Scandinavia to Britain have been picked up on radar screens flying at heights of 4.3 miles (7 kilometers).

Before they were killed by settlers, 30 million bison used to **migrate** across the prairies of North America every fall in search of fresh grass. Their hooves wore paths so deep and wide that people were able to use the ruts as roads.

Manatees like to live in warm water. They are more likely to catch diseases if they become too cold. In winter, if the water temperature falls below 68°F, they migrate to warmer areas, such as natural springs, or places where power plants pump out heated waste water.

The world's oldest known living wild bird, a 50 year-old Manx shearwater, has probably migrated farther than any other animal. Each year it flies 10,000 miles (16,000 kilometers) from Great Britain to Argentina then across North America back to Britain. All its migrations add up to about 497,100 miles (800,000 kilometers)—about the same as flying twenty times around Earth. The migration plus all other trips add up to almost 5 million miles (8 million kilometers), which is like flying to the Moon and back ten times.

A salmon remembers the exact taste and smell of the river where it was born. Even in the deep ocean, it can pick up the smell of its home hundreds of miles away. When it is ready to **mate,** the salmon "follows its nose" all the way back to where it was born.

When migrating swans are ready to take off, they need to let the whole flock know. The trumpeter swan bobs its head and neck up and down, and makes a loud trumpet sound.

Every summer, 20 million female free-tailed bats leave their home in Mexico and migrate north. They all head for Bracken Cave in Texas, almost 1,000 miles (1,600 kilometers) away. Nobody knows why the females choose this cave so far away from home.

Glossary

antenna   (more than one are called antennae) long, thin feeler located on the head. Lobsters have two antennae.

breeding ground   place where animals **mate** and raise their young

breeding season   time of year when animals mate

coral reef   underwater formation made of the hard skeletons of millions of tiny sea animals

current   flowing water or air

dormant   not active

drought   long period without rain

estuary   stretch of water where a river flows into the sea

fat reserves   extra energy stored in the body, allowing an animal to live for long periods without food

habitat   place where an animal or plant lives

hibernate   sleep through the winter

infestation   attack by a large number of pests, such as caterpillars

irruption   sudden, unexpected invasion

magnetic   acting like a magnet

magnetic field   force around Earth that pulls magnetic objects in a certain direction

mammal   animal that feeds on its mother's milk

mate   partner. Also, what a male and female animal do to start an egg or baby growing inside the female.

migrate   move from one place to another

migration   the act of moving from one place to another

monsoon   seasonal wind that brings a long period of heavy rain

native species   type of plant or animal that has always been found in a particular place

nectar   sugary liquid made by flowers

nomadic migration   movement in search of food that does not follow a pattern

offspring   children

plague   outbreak of pests or disease that spreads over a large area

removal migration   movement to avoid overcrowding or starvation

spawn   lay groups of eggs in the water

thermal   rising current of warm air

tundra   cold, flat area in the Arctic that has no trees and is covered by snow for about half the year

Further Reading

Bredeson, Carmen. *Animals That Migrate.* New York: Franklin Watts, 2002.

McDonnell, Janet. *Animal Migration.* Chanhassen, Minn.: Child's World, 1998.

Riha, Susanne. *Animal Journeys: Life Cycles and Migrations.* San Diego: Blackbirch Press, 1999.

Simon, Seymour. *They Swim the Seas: The Mystery of Animal Migration.* San Diego: Browndeer Press, 1998.

Index